"Everyone has a gift for something, even if it is that of being a good friend. Young people should try and set a goal for themselves, and see that everything they do has relation to the ultimate attainment of the goal."

—MARIAN ANDERSON

MARIAN ANDERSON

BY JAMES MEADOWS

The Child's World®

COVER PHOTO

Portrait of Marian Anderson
Courtesy of the University of Pennsylvania

Published in the United States of America by The Child's World®, Inc.
PO Box 326
Chanhassen, MN 55317-0326
800-599-READ
www.childsworld.com

Product Manager Mary Francis-DeMarois/The Creative Spark
Designer Robert E. Bonaker/Graphic Design & Consulting Co.
Editorial Direction Elizabeth Sirimarco Budd
Contributors Mary Berendes, Red Line Editorial, Katherine Stevenson, Ph.D.

The Child's World®, Inc., and Journey to Freedom® are the sole property
and registered trademarks of The Child's World®, Inc.

Library of Congress Cataloging-in-Publication Data
Meadows, James, 1969–
Marian Anderson / by James Meadows.
p. cm.
Includes bibliographical references and index.
ISBN 1-56766-921-2 (alk. paper)
1. Anderson, Marian, 1897–1993—Juvenile literature.
2. Contraltos—United States—Biography—Juvenile literature.
3. African American singers—Biography—Juvenile literature.
[1. Anderson, Marian, 1897–1993. 2. Singers. 3. Women—Biography.
4. African Americans—Biography.] I. Title.
ML3930.A5 M45 2001
782.1'092—dc21

2001001074

Contents

A Grand Farewell

Marian Anderson ended her career as a concert singer in 1965. At 68 years old, she gave her farewell **recital** in one of the most famous music halls in the world: New York City's Carnegie Hall. She was an international star, known all over the world as one of the greatest classical singers of all time. Her voice was so strong, it could fill entire concert halls. It was so expressive, it could move audiences to tears or to shouts of joy. Marian Anderson's voice was legendary.

Anderson was one of the world's greatest concert singers, but she was also much more. She worked to become one of the world's best-known singers at a time when African Americans faced terrible **discrimination.** When she began her singing career in the 1920s, **segregation** was a fact of life for black people in the United States. This system of separation made it difficult for them to work in high-paying or desirable professions—including careers in classical music.

When Marian Anderson began her career, few African Americans earned their living as concert singers, and none of them were at the top of the profession. At that time, African Americans were not even allowed to attend most music schools. Few black people dreamed of singing classical music, no matter how much talent they had.

Anderson became an international celebrity because she was the most talented singer of her generation. But her achievements went beyond the success she found on stage. Anderson also broke through barriers of **racism.** She remained optimistic no matter what difficulties she encountered. She faced discrimination with dignity, reminding Americans of what it meant to be human.

University of Pennsylvania

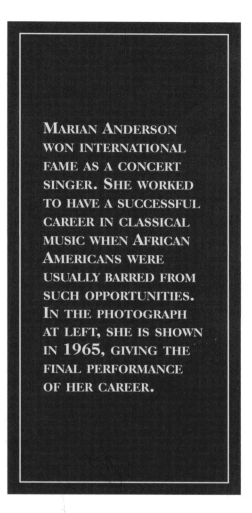

MARIAN ANDERSON WON INTERNATIONAL FAME AS A CONCERT SINGER. SHE WORKED TO HAVE A SUCCESSFUL CAREER IN CLASSICAL MUSIC WHEN AFRICAN AMERICANS WERE USUALLY BARRED FROM SUCH OPPORTUNITIES. IN THE PHOTOGRAPH AT LEFT, SHE IS SHOWN IN 1965, GIVING THE FINAL PERFORMANCE OF HER CAREER.

When Anderson performed her last concert in 1965, she made the front page of the *New York Times,* the most respected newspaper in the United States. A reporter from that paper wrote, "Her appearance was not so much as a singer than as a legend, not so much as a Negro **contralto** than as a regal and majestic celebrity." Marian Anderson had tremendous talent, but her life off stage was as great as her concert career.

MARIAN ANDERSON WAS BORN ON FEBRUARY 17, 1897. SHE WAS THE FIRST OF JOHN AND ANNA ANDERSON'S THREE DAUGHTERS. THE ANDERSONS DID NOT HAVE MUCH MONEY, BUT MARIAN NEVER FELT POOR BECAUSE SHE CAME FROM A LOVING FAMILY.

A Little Girl with a Big Voice

Marian Anderson first dreamed of becoming a singer as a young child in South Philadelphia. The oldest of three daughters, she was born on February 17, 1897. Marian loved her parents very much. Although the family never had much money, her parents took good care of the girls. Her father, John, supported the family by selling ice. Her mother, Anna, stayed home to care for the girls. Marian's father always provided his family with food and shelter. When she was old enough, Marian earned extra money for the family by scrubbing the neighbors' stairs and sidewalks.

Marian was a happy child. She laughed and sang at home and enjoyed sitting in the kitchen chatting with her mother. By age six, Marian had joined the junior choir at her church. It was in this choir that Marian first discovered her love of music. She and another young singer learned a **duet** and sang it in front of the entire church. It was Marian's first performance.

Marian also enjoyed singing with her class at school. Even when she was young, her voice was strong and beautiful. Marian's father recognized her talent and bought a piano. The family didn't have enough money for lessons, so Marian and her sisters taught themselves to play simple melodies. One day, Marian walked down the street and saw an African American woman playing the piano. Until then, Marian thought that playing music was something only white people could do. Marian realized that if that African American woman could be a musician, so could she. She continued to work at playing piano and grew better and better at it. She also began to dream of becoming a singer.

When Marian was 13 years old, tragedy struck her family. At Christmastime in 1910, Marian's father was accidentally struck in the head at work. He lay sick through the holidays and died a short time later. Everything changed after that.

Marian and her family moved into her grandmother's house. Marian's mother went to work to support her daughters. Marian gave up school for a while to help support the family as well. She didn't start high school until 1918, when she enrolled at South Philadelphia High School for Girls.

Although the death of her father was a sad period in Marian's life, it did not lessen her love of music. In fact, that love grew stronger with time. With her mother's support, Marian was able to pursue her talent. She began to sing more and more in church and then at school. Her low, rich voice continued to turn heads and win praise.

In 1910, Marian (seated at center) posed for this photograph with her mother, Anna (top) and her sisters, Alyse (left) and Ethel (right). Sadly, the family faced great tragedy that year when John Anderson died, leaving Anna to support their three daughters.

Singing was serious business for Marian, even when she was a teenager. In the church choir, she often learned all the parts for a song, not just her own. She learned the **solos** as well. If a soloist was absent, the choir **conductor** could call on Marian to sing the part at a moment's notice. Performing in front of a crowd didn't scare Marian. She loved to sing, especially at her church. It was through her church that she met a well-known singer named Roland Hayes.

Roland Hayes was one of the few African Americans at the time who was trained to sing classical music. He sang songs in different languages and traveled to foreign countries. He was the first to notice Marian's great talent. Hayes told her family that she could be a **professional** singer and needed to take lessons.

Marian soon began singing at other churches in Philadelphia. Her soaring voice won invitations to sing at other community events, too. It wasn't long before she began charging a small fee for her appearances. Marian continued to get invitations to sing, but she knew that Roland Hayes was right. She needed training to become a true professional singer. Singing classical music is different from many other kinds of singing. Classical singers must learn to fill an entire auditorium with their voice without using a microphone. They must train their voices to flow smoothly, like a river, or stop suddenly, like a raindrop hitting the ground. They must learn to sing higher and lower than what feels comfortable at first.

University of Pennsylvania

AS A YOUNG GIRL, MARIAN'S BEAUTIFUL VOICE EARNED HER INVITATIONS TO PERFORM AT CHURCH SERVICES AND SPECIAL EVENTS IN PHILADELPHIA. SHE BEGAN HER PROFESSIONAL CAREER BY CHARGING FIVE DOLLARS FOR EACH PERFORMANCE. AFTER EVERY RECITAL, MARIAN KEPT JUST ONE DOLLAR FOR HERSELF. SHE GAVE THE REST OF THE MONEY TO HER SISTERS AND MOTHER.

Classical music is also very precise. The songs are written down on paper with musical notes. Each note is a sound, and each sound is sung in a particular way. A classical singer must learn to sing hundreds of songs just as they are written. In addition, most classical songs and **operas** are written in languages other than English, including French, German, and Italian. A great singer must learn to sing in these languages, pronouncing the words perfectly. It takes years of difficult training for someone to master all the skills needed to sing classical music. With training, all of these things become easier.

Marian could get such training at a music school. While she was a teenager, she visited a school in Philadelphia, hoping to find out if she could enroll there. She waited patiently in line to talk to someone at the school. When Marian's turn came, the young white woman behind the desk called on the person behind Marian. She continued to ignore Marian until everyone else had been served. When there was no one else in line, the woman said, "What do you want?"

Marian politely explained that she had questions about entering the music school. The woman looked at Marian coldly and said, "We don't take colored." Marian was deeply hurt by this woman's racism. She later wrote about the experience:

I don't think I said a word. I just looked at this girl and was shocked that such words could come from one so young. If she had been old and sour faced, I might not have been startled. I cannot say why her youth shocked me as much as her words.... I could not conceive of a person surrounded as she was with the joy that is music without having some sense of its beauty rub off on her. I did not argue with her or ask to see her superior. It was as if a cold horrifying hand had been laid on me. I turned and walked out.

It was years before Marian would even speak of this incident to anyone but her mother. This Philadelphia music school was not the only school to bar African Americans. At that time, many schools in the United States were segregated.

Marian decided not to try to enroll at other schools. She didn't want to risk rejection again. Marian's experience with racism affected her throughout her life. Even after she became a world-famous singer, she wished she could have attended a music school to perfect her singing.

The music school incident was not Marian's only experience with racism. As she began to perform in other cities, she often traveled by train. Every time she traveled, she worried that there would be some problem with her travel arrangements. Sometimes ticket attendants on trains would not give her a seat, even when space was available. When she arrived at her destination, some hotels would not let her sleep in their rooms. She faced such racism even after she became famous. Marian suffered these **humiliations** because, as an African American, she had little choice. She also hoped that her behavior might change some peoples' views about African Americans.

Marian Anderson didn't let racism stop her from becoming a professional singer. Even though she couldn't attend music school, she found excellent private teachers who wanted to work with her. In 1915, Marian met her first voice teacher, Mary Saunders Patterson. Patterson taught Marian how to control her voice. Marian was a fast learner and soon knew all that Patterson could teach her. In 1916, Marian found another teacher, Agnes Reifsnyder. Reifsnyder introduced Marian to many new pieces of music and helped her prepare for her first out-of-town performances.

Marian's third teacher was her most important. His name was Giuseppe Boghetti. Boghetti was an excellent singer. He was also a famous voice instructor. Marian's high school principal arranged her first audition with Boghetti. When he entered the room, Boghetti said right away that he had no time to take on a new student and was only listening to Marian as a favor. But as soon as he heard Marian sing the African American **spiritual** "Deep River," he changed his mind.

University of Pennsylvania

MARIAN ANDERSON HAD DIFFICULTY FINDING A SCHOOL
WHERE SHE COULD ENROLL IN MUSIC CLASSES. SHE BEGAN
TAKING PRIVATE SINGING LESSONS AT AGE 18 WHEN A FAMILY
FRIEND TOOK HER TO THE STUDIO OF A SINGER NAMED MARY
SAUNDERS PATTERSON. THE ANDERSONS COULD NOT AFFORD
TO PAY FOR LESSONS, SO PATTERSON OFFERED TO TEACH THE
YOUNG SINGER FOR FREE.

oghetti knew right away that Marian had great talent. "I will need only two years with you," he told her. "After that you will be able to go anywhere and sing for anybody." After they began working together, Boghetti was Marian's teacher until he died in 1941.

Boghetti wanted Marian to begin her lessons immediately. There was only one problem: Marian had no money to pay him. Her neighbors and the people of the Union Baptist Church came to the rescue. They held a concert that raised about $600—enough for Marian to begin lessons.

University of Pennsylvania

MARIAN IS SHOWN HERE (CIRCLED) WITH THE 1921 GRADUATING CLASS OF SOUTH PHILADELPHIA HIGH SCHOOL FOR GIRLS. MARIAN WAS OLDER THAN MANY OF HER CLASSMATES WHEN SHE GRADUATED BECAUSE SHE HAD TAKEN TIME OFF TO HELP SUPPORT HER FAMILY. HER SINGING CAREER HAD ALSO TAKEN AWAY TIME FROM HER STUDIES.

University of Pennsylvania

IN 1918, THE MEMBERS OF MARIAN'S CHURCH RAISED MONEY TO HELP HER PAY FOR LESSONS WITH FAMED TEACHER GIUSEPPE BOGHETTI (ABOVE). BOGHETTI WAS THE MOST IMPORTANT TEACHER OF MARIAN'S CAREER. SHE WORKED WITH HIM UNTIL HIS DEATH IN 1941.

Early Disappointment

Under Boghetti's instruction, Marian gained a **reputation** as a fine singer. She traveled to colleges to give special concerts. She sang for the National Association for the Advancement of Colored People (NAACP) and the National Baptist Convention. She also continued to sing at churches. Marian regularly sold out these concerts, which means that every available ticket was sold. Audiences were thrilled to hear her sing.

Marian felt confident that she could become a great artist. In 1924, she decided to take a risk. She prepared to sing a recital at New York City's Town Hall, a **prestigious** concert hall. Marian knew she would attract the attention of serious musicians and important music **critics** if she sang there. If the music critics liked her performance, they would write positive newspaper articles about her. This would help her establish a successful career. Marian knew she had to impress the critics for her concert to be a success.

Marian worked tirelessly on her music. She chose very difficult songs. She had sung some of them at other concerts in the past, but four songs by the **composer** Brahms were new to her. Boghetti reassured Marian that everything would be fine, but she had her doubts.

On the day of the concert, Marian did exactly what Boghetti had told her to do. She ate at four o'clock in the afternoon so she wouldn't be too hungry or too full during the concert. She arrived at the hall at seven o'clock for the eight o'clock show. She waited anxiously as her performance time approached. Eight o'clock came and went. Forty-five minutes later, Marian was told to begin her performance. What had caused the delay, she wondered?

When Marian walked on stage and looked into the audience, she knew why they had delayed her show. The hall was almost empty! The concert manager was waiting to see if more people would arrive late.

University of Pennsylvania

songs were written in German. Marian had practiced the German pronunciation, but she did not know what all the words meant. She struggled through each of the songs. She thought they would never end. When the concert was over, she knew it had not been her best performance.

The music critics shared her opinion. Their reviews were not very positive, and Marian felt like a failure. She was ashamed to have stepped into the spotlight before she was truly ready. She returned to Philadelphia wanting to give up singing altogether. After a short time, though, Marian got over her disappointment and began to sing again. She was determined never again to appear on stage unprepared.

Marian was heartbroken. This was the most important concert of her young career, but almost no one had come to see her.

To make matters worse, Marian had a difficult time with the four new Brahms songs. The **lyrics** to these

Marian Anderson's determination paid off quickly. In 1925, she entered a New York Philharmonic voice contest and won first prize among 300 contestants. Critics praised her performance, and Marian knew her dreams might still come true. The Town Hall concert had taught Marian an important lesson. She knew she had to learn the foreign languages she would sing as a classical performer. The best way to do that was to travel to Europe. Going to Europe was another risk, but it was one she knew she must take.

MARIAN ANDERSON ONCE GAVE A CONCERT IN A SMALL NEBRASKA COLLEGE TOWN. A STUDENT WHO WAS WORKING HER WAY THROUGH COLLEGE COULD NOT GET TIME OFF FROM HER JOB AT THE LOCAL HOTEL TO SEE THE CONCERT. MARIAN WAS STAYING AT THE HOTEL. AFTER HER PERFORMANCE, SHE ENTERED THE HOTEL LOBBY. THE STUDENT ASKED ABOUT THE CONCERT AND SAID HOW DISAPPOINTED SHE WAS NOT TO HAVE BEEN THERE. RIGHT THERE IN THE HOTEL LOBBY, WITHOUT A PIANO TO ACCOMPANY HER, MARIAN SANG FOR THE STUDENT.

The European Tours

Marian Anderson's 1928 trip to Europe was the first of many. She used her savings to buy a ticket for a ship that took her to London, England. Marian did not give many performances on this first trip to Europe. She met a few good teachers and studied German. When she ran out of money, it was time to go home.

After she returned, Marian soon realized that her career was going nowhere in the United States. White American audiences would not attend classical music performances given by an African American. In 1930, Marian decided to go back to Europe, where things would be different. Her mother and sisters supported her decision to return, although they would miss her. They knew she would stay away longer this time.

Marian lived in Germany for six months. She stayed with a German family named the von Erdbergs. They spoke no English, and Marian spoke almost no German. Living with the von Erdbergs was awkward for Marian at first, but it did help her learn German quickly. Soon after she arrived, Marian met two men who would help her career. Rulle Rasmussen was a musician's manager from Norway. His friend, Kosti Vehanen, was a classical pianist from Finland. The two men were in Germany looking for talented singers. When they met Marian, they asked if she would travel to Norway to perform. Marian said yes. She had no idea how important this trip would be.

Marian traveled to Norway planning to sing only six concerts. But after her second performance, everyone wanted to hear the talented American sing. Rasmussen and Vehanen scheduled more concerts in Norway as well as in the other Scandinavian countries of Sweden, Finland, and Denmark. The Scandinavian people loved Marian! They sent her letters, flowers, and gifts. She was thrilled by her success.

MARIAN ANDERSON'S
CAREER BEGAN TO
BLOSSOM IN EUROPE,
WHERE AUDIENCES
WERE MORE CON-
CERNED WITH HER
GREAT TALENT THAN
WITH THE COLOR OF
HER SKIN.

University of Pennsylvania

University of Pennsylvania

Of her success in Europe, Marian said, "It made me realize that the time and energy invested in seeking to become an artist were worthwhile, and that what I had dared to aspire to was not impossible."

Many of Anderson's new admirers had never met an African American person, but they did not respond with **prejudice.** Most were curious, respectful, and admiring. They wanted to talk to Marian to find out what it was like to be an African American. They looked beyond the color of her skin to see who she really was: a talented young woman with a bright future ahead of her. Marian's first Scandinavian tour helped her career in Europe. It also strengthened her hope that people of different races could get along. Sadly, when she returned to the United States, little had changed. Her talent still earned little recognition in her own country.

Marian made a third trip to Europe in 1933. This time, she stayed for two years—and what a time she had! Scandinavian audiences were even more enthusiastic than before. Marian performed more than a hundred concerts in 12 months. Kosti Vehanen accompanied her on the piano, as he would continue to do for the next 10 years. Marian received rave reviews from critics, learned songs in new languages, and met the best musicians and composers in Europe. Marian Anderson was a star. One Swedish newspaper called her success "Marian Fever."

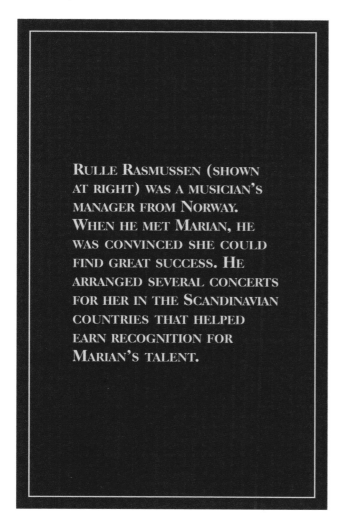

RULLE RASMUSSEN (SHOWN AT RIGHT) WAS A MUSICIAN'S MANAGER FROM NORWAY. WHEN HE MET MARIAN, HE WAS CONVINCED SHE COULD FIND GREAT SUCCESS. HE ARRANGED SEVERAL CONCERTS FOR HER IN THE SCANDINAVIAN COUNTRIES THAT HELPED EARN RECOGNITION FOR MARIAN'S TALENT.

University of Pennsylvania

Marian Anderson performed all over Europe. She sang for religious leaders and kings. In Austria, she sang for an audience that included Arturo Toscanini, one of the greatest orchestra conductors of all time. When Toscanini heard Marian's voice, he said that hers was a voice heard only once in a hundred years. When others learned about Toscanini's compliment, even more people wanted to hear Marian sing.

Wherever Marian sang, she gave a wonderful performance. Her great success inspired her to do her very best. But the most important part of her trip was when she met a music manager named Sol Hurok. A good manager can be the key to an artist's success. Concert halls often ask an artist to give a concert based on a manager's excellent reputation. Sol Hurok had such a reputation. The owners of concert halls knew his artists were the very best and would bring large audiences. With Sol Hurok behind her, Marian had a chance to break the color barrier that had long held her back in the United States.

University of Pennsylvania

MARIAN ANDERSON IS SHOWN HERE PERFORMING FOR AN AUDIENCE IN VIENNA, AUSTRIA. AT THE PIANO IS KOSTI VEHANEN. AFTER MEETING MARIAN IN THE EARLY 1930s, VEHANEN PERFORMED WITH HER FOR MANY YEARS.

University of Pennsylvania

MARIAN ANDERSON'S SUCCESS IN EUROPE ENCOURAGED HER
TO DREAM OF AN EQUALLY IMPRESSIVE CAREER IN HER OWN
COUNTRY. WHEN SHE MET MANAGER SOL HUROK, IT SEEMED
AS IF SHE MIGHT BE ABLE TO MAKE THIS DREAM COME TRUE.

University of Pennsylvania

SOL HUROK TURNED OUT
TO BE AN EXCELLENT
MANAGER FOR ANDERSON,
HELPING HER BUILD A
CAREER IN THE UNITED
STATES. SHE ADMIRED
WHAT SHE CALLED "THE
BOLDNESS WITH WHICH
HE DID THINGS." HUROK
ENCOURAGED ANDERSON
TO CONCENTRATE ON HER
SINGING RATHER THAN
ON BUSINESS MATTERS
OR THE RACISM SHE
CONTINUED TO FACE.

Coming Home

Sol Hurok took a big risk when he agreed to manage Marian Anderson. No one doubted her skill and talent, but she was an African American. No African American singer had gained popularity with white audiences in the United States. All that changed when Marian returned home in 1935.

Marian sang her homecoming concert at New York City's Town Hall, the site of her great disappointment 11 years earlier. This time, many people came to hear her sing. The concert was a success, and the critics loved her. Her reputation in Europe finally began to reach people in her own country. Marian's success continued outside of New York City as well. She began a series of concerts that eventually took her to more than 600 U.S. cities.

Marian was a star, but no amount of success could protect her from racism. Hotels and restaurants that barred African Americans often denied her service. The worst incident of racism took place in 1939. She and Sol Hurok thought it was time for her to sing in a major concert hall in the nation's capital city, Washington, D.C. They tried to book Constitution Hall, a large, well-known auditorium owned by a women's group called the Daughters of the American Revolution (DAR).

The DAR refused to let Marian sing at Constitution Hall because she was black. Her talent and skill did not matter, nor did her reputation in Europe. Not even Sol Hurok's efforts could change their minds. The DAR stuck firmly to its decision.

Eleanor Roosevelt, wife of President Franklin Delano Roosevelt, had spent her life defending people who faced discrimination and **injustice.** She was also a member of the DAR. She publicly demanded that Marian Anderson be allowed to sing at Constitution Hall.

When the DAR refused, Roosevelt gave up her membership in the organization. The DAR's act of discrimination turned into a national **controversy.**

Eleanor Roosevelt and many others in the U.S. government supported Marian Anderson. They could not make the DAR open its doors to Marian, but they could arrange another concert for her. On Easter Sunday of 1939, Marian Anderson sang in front of the Lincoln Memorial in Washington, D.C. More than 75,000 people filled the Mall to listen to her. Millions more listened to the performance on the radio.

University of Pennsylvania

A CROWD OF **75,000** PEOPLE CAME TO HEAR MARIAN ANDERSON SING AT THE LINCOLN MEMORIAL ON APRIL **9,** 1939.

Marian Anderson's concert marked an important moment in history. She was a powerful figure in a great challenge to segregation. After the controversy died down, the DAR changed its rules and allowed people of color to perform in Constitution Hall.

Marian continued to fight racism. She later refused to sing for segregated audiences. Because of Marian's stand, some concert halls changed their seating rules, allowing African Americans to attend or to sit in the same areas as white people. When world-famous Marian Anderson came to stay, some hotels changed their policy of barring African Americans for her—and then for other African Americans as well. Marian was more than an extraordinary singer. She was a model of courage and dignity for the world, and she was rewarded for that part of her life as well. In 1939, the NAACP awarded her the Spingarn Medal, an important achievement award given to African Americans.

University of Pennsylvania

AMONG THE MANY HONORS MARIAN RECEIVED WAS THE SPINGARN MEDAL. ELEANOR ROOSEVELT (LEFT) PRESENTED HER WITH THE AWARD IN 1939. OVER THE YEARS, MARIAN RECEIVED SEVERAL SIGNIFICANT HONORS FOR HER ACHIEVEMENTS. IN 1963, SHE WAS AWARDED THE PRESIDENTIAL MEDAL OF FREEDOM, AND IN 1978 SHE WON THE CONGRESSIONAL GOLD MEDAL. IN 1991, TWO YEARS BEFORE HER DEATH, MARIAN WON A GRAMMY LIFETIME ACHIEVEMENT AWARD.

Marian Anderson's singing career continued to climb. She sang at the White House for the Roosevelts. In later years, she also performed for presidents Dwight Eisenhower, John Kennedy, and Lyndon Johnson. Beginning in the late 1940s, Marian began traveling all over the world. She returned to Scandinavia. She also performed in other European countries and in South America, Jamaica, the West Indies, Japan, Southeast Asia, China, Israel, Morocco, and Tunisia. Marian was popular with audiences worldwide.

Her travels and extraordinary talent made her one of the most celebrated singers in the world. Although she did not like making recordings, the few she did make sold more than a million copies.

In January of 1955, Marian Anderson performed with the prestigious Metropolitan Opera Company in New York City. She was the first African American to appear with that respected organization. In some ways, it was the high point of her singing career.

University of Pennsylvania

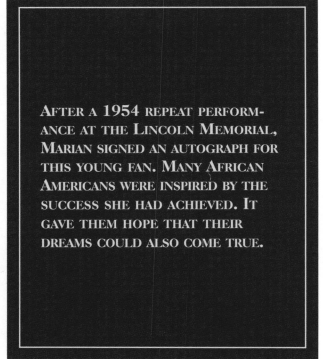

AFTER A 1954 REPEAT PERFORMANCE AT THE LINCOLN MEMORIAL, MARIAN SIGNED AN AUTOGRAPH FOR THIS YOUNG FAN. MANY AFRICAN AMERICANS WERE INSPIRED BY THE SUCCESS SHE HAD ACHIEVED. IT GAVE THEM HOPE THAT THEIR DREAMS COULD ALSO COME TRUE.

University of Pennsylvania

In January of 1955, Marian Anderson became the first African American to perform with the Metropolitan Opera Company. She is shown here in her role as the fortuneteller in the Italian opera, *Un Ballo in Maschera* (which means "A Masked Ball").

arian Anderson was nearly 58 years old at the time. Her voice was no longer at its peak, but her appearance once again opened doors to many young singers of color. The *New York Times* wrote about the historic event, noting "that she has fulfilled a lifelong ambition is not nearly so important as the fact that we will have an opportunity to hear her.… Whenever there was 'discrimination' against Miss Anderson the real suffering was not hers but ours. It was we who were impoverished, not she."

Marian had traveled a world away from South Philadelphia, but she always found her way home. In 1954, she founded the Marian Anderson Recreation Center in South Philadelphia. She did this to thank many of her old neighbors and friends who helped her at the beginning of her career. Marian also supported other young singers just starting their careers. She established a **scholarship** contest for young singers who might not have the chance to study music without help.

Marian left the world of bright lights and travel in 1965 after giving her farewell performance at Carnegie Hall. She settled down with her husband, Orpheus Fisher, whom she had married in 1943. They lived on a farm in Connecticut until Fisher's death in 1992. Then Marian moved to Portland, Oregon, to live with her nephew, James DePriest. She died there on April 8, 1993, at 96 years of age.

Marian Anderson lives on in the careers of other world-famous African American concert singers. Leontyne Price, Jessye Norman, and Kathleen Battle all remember Marian Anderson as their musical inspiration. But who can say how many other people she has inspired? Marian Anderson was a pioneer, a woman who dared to dream of what others thought impossible. She encouraged white Americans to look beyond skin color to see African Americans as beautiful, dignified, and talented. Today she inspires all who know her story to be the best and to achieve whatever they may dream.

University of Pennsylvania

In 1990, several important performers from the world of classical music gathered to honor Marian Anderson. She is shown here (in front) with two of the African American singers she inspired: Jessye Norman (left) and Kathleen Battle (right). Standing in the center is James Levine, conductor of the Metropolitan Opera Company.

Timeline

1897	Marian Anderson is born in South Philadelphia on February 17.
1903	Six-year-old Marian gives her first performance at her family's church.
1915	Young Marian begins studying with music teacher Mary Saunders Patterson.
1916	Marian starts studying with another teacher, Agnes Reifsnyder.
1918	Marian begins high school at South Philadelphia High School for Girls. She meets Giuseppe Boghetti, who will be her music instructor until his death in 1941.
1921	Marian graduates from high school.
1924	After giving a disappointing recital at New York City's Town Hall, Marian realizes that she must study foreign languages to succeed as a classical singer.
1925	Marian enters a New York Philharmonic voice competition and wins first prize.
1928	Marian travels to Europe for the first time.
1930	On a second trip to Europe, Marian meets pianist Kosti Vehanen and manager Rulle Rasmussen. They help her book concerts in Scandinavia, where she tours for six months. For the next 10 years, Vehanen will accompany her on the piano at her concerts.
1933	On a third trip to Europe, Anderson impresses audiences across the continent, performing more than a hundred concerts in 12 months.
1935	After two years in Europe, Anderson returns to the United States and finds success with her new manager, Sol Hurok. She will work with Hurok for the remainder of her career. Anderson performs once again at New York City's Town Hall, and the concert is a great success.
1939	The Daughters of the American Revolution (DAR) bars Anderson from singing in Constitution Hall because she is African American. Eleanor Roosevelt and others in the United States government come to Anderson's defense. On Easter Sunday, Anderson gives a public concert at the Lincoln Memorial to a live audience of 75,000 people. Millions more listen on the radio.
	The National Association for the Advancement of Colored People (NAACP) awards Marian Anderson its Spingarn Medal. Eleanor Roosevelt presents the award.
1943	Anderson marries Orpheus Fisher.
1940s –1950s	Anderson travels in Europe, Asia, and Africa, giving hundreds of performances to people of different races and cultures. She becomes one of the most popular concert singers in the United States.
1954	Anderson opens the Marian Anderson Recreation Center in South Philadelphia.
1955	On January 7, Anderson becomes the first African American to perform with the prestigious Metropolitan Opera Company in New York City.
1963	Anderson is awarded the Presidential Medal of Freedom.
1965	At 68 years of age, Anderson gives her farewell recital at Carnegie Hall in New York City.
1978	Anderson is awarded the Congressional Gold Medal.
1984	Anderson is awarded the Eleanor Roosevelt Human Rights Award.
1991	Anderson wins the Grammy Lifetime Achievement Award.
1993	Marian Anderson dies in Portland, Oregon.

Glossary

composer (kom-POHZ-er)
A composer is a person who writes pieces of music. Marian Anderson performed four songs by the composer Brahms at her first Town Hall recital.

conductor (kun-DUK-ter)
A conductor leads the performers in an orchestra or choir, training them to work together and keeping time for them. The church choir conductor often asked Marian Anderson to sing.

contralto (kun-TRAHL-toh)
A contralto is a person with a singing voice higher than that of a tenor and lower than that of a mezzo-soprano. Marian Anderson was a contralto.

controversy (KON-truh-ver-see)
A controversy is a dispute or argument. A national controversy arose when the Daughters of the American Revolution would not let Marian Anderson sing at Constitution Hall.

critics (KRIT-iks)
Critics comment on what is good or bad about music, books, pictures, or other works of art. Marian Anderson knew she would attract the attention of music critics if she performed at New York City's Town Hall.

discrimination (dis-krim-ih-NAY-shun)
Discrimination is the unfair treatment of people simply because they are different. Marian Anderson worked to become a well-known singer at a time when African Americans faced discrimination.

duet (doo-ET)
A duet is a piece of music for two voices or instruments. At age six, Marian Anderson and another young singer performed a duet at her church.

humiliations (hyoo-mil-ee-AY-shuns)
Humiliations are things that damage a person's pride, dignity, or self-respect. Marian Anderson suffered certain humiliations because she was an African American.

injustice (in-JUSS-tiss)
Injustice is something that is unfair or wrong. Eleanor Roosevelt spent her life defending people who faced discrimination and injustice.

lyrics (LEER-iks)
Lyrics are the words to a song. Marian Anderson sang some lyrics in French, German, and Italian.

Glossary

operas (OP-er-uhz)
Operas are plays sung to music. Most operas are written in languages other than English.

prejudice (PREH-juh-diss)
Prejudice is a negative feeling or opinion about someone without a good reason. Scandinavian audiences were not prejudiced toward Marian Anderson because of her skin color.

prestigious (pres-TEEJ-us)
If something is prestigious, it is considered valuable or important. The Metropolitan Opera Company is a prestigious organization.

professional (proh-FESH-un-ull)
A professional is someone who uses a talent or skill to earn a living. Marian Anderson was a professional singer.

racism (RAY-sih-zim)
Racism is a negative feeling or opinion about people because of their race. Marian Anderson broke through barriers of racism.

recital (ree-SY-tul)
A recital is a musical performance. Marian Anderson gave her farewell recital at Carnegie Hall in New York City.

reputation (rep-yoo-TAY-shun)
A person's reputation is what others think and say about that person. Marian Anderson gained a reputation as a fine singer.

scholarship (SKOL-er-ship)
A scholarship is money awarded to a student to help pay for his or her education. Marian Anderson established a scholarship contest for young singers.

segregation (seh-greh-GAY-shun)
Segregation is the practice of keeping people separate. In the 1920s, segregation made it difficult for black people in the United States to work in high-paying or desirable jobs.

solos (SOH-lohz)
Solos are pieces of music performed by a single voice or instrument. The choir conductor at Marian's church often asked her to sing solos.

spiritual (SPEER-ih-chewl)
Spirituals are religious songs that originated among African Americans in the southern United States. Marian Anderson often sang spirituals at her recitals.

Index

Index

Further Information

Books and Magazines

Livingston, Myra Cohn. *Keep on Singing: A Ballad of Marian Anderson.* New York: Holiday House, 1994.

McKissack, Pat, Patricia McKissack, and Frederick McKissack. *Marian Anderson: A Great Singer* (Great African Americans series). Springfield, NJ: Enslow Publishers, 2001.

McNair, James. *Leontyne Price* (Journey to Freedom series). Chanhassen, MN: The Child's World, 2001.

Rosenberg, J. *Sing Me a Song.* London: Thames & Hudson, 1996.

Tedards, Anne. *Marian Anderson* (American Women of Achievement). Broomall, PA: Chelsea House, 1989.

Web Sites

Visit the University of Pennsylvania's Internet exhibition on Marian Anderson:
http://www.library.upenn.edu/special/gallery/anderson/

Visit the PBS Web site to read a news story about Marian Anderson:
http://www.pbs.org/newshour/bb/remember/1997/anderson_2-26a.html

Listen to Marian Anderson sing and to excerpts from an interview with her:
http://www.library.upenn.edu/special/gallery/anderson/av/int01b.ram

Read brief biographies of Marian Anderson:
http://www.afrovoices.com/anderson.html
http://kennedy-center.org/programs/family/mariananderson/woman.html

Visit the Web site of New York's Metropolitan Opera Company:
http://www.metopera.org/home.html

Read the story of *Un Ballo in Maschera:*
http://www.metopera.org/synopses/forza.html